# Poems 2/3

Michael Boy works as a writer and
conceptual artist. He explores the
feelings and peculiarities of special
people and tries to capture moments
through poetry. An approach and a
confrontation.

These poems are dedicated to
Birgit, Max and Leo.

Bibliografische Information der
Deutschen Nationalbibliothek: Die
Deutsche Nationalbibliothek
verzeichnet diese Publikation in der
Deutschen Nationalbibliografie;
detaillierte bibliografische Daten sind
im Internet über dnb.dnb.de abrufbar.

Herstellung und Verlag:
BoD – Books on Demand,
Norderstedt

ISBN: 9783753453880

96 crazy short poems from the main volume "Poems".

Incomprehensible poems by and about special people. In search of encounters, self-discovery and self-help as a mixture of words. An affair of the heart.

Part 2

We come to the 2nd part. Further 96
poems follow. Some poems resemble
each other and are spun on in the
following associated poem or also
dissolved. In the whole book always 3
poems belong together. However,
these were well mixed by me. It is not
necessary to go consciously on the
search. By chance one will come across
it, or not.

1.  Prison
Having life locked up
very securely
in the prison of dreams.


2.  Love
In the thirst for love forget the self,
think good
and ask.


3.  Ask
And we ask and pray,
poetry stories
and again be in the prison of dreams,
in the prison of love.

4.  Morning
A good morning brings back hope,
a good day makes you forget dying for
a moment,
it will be a good day.


5.  Born again
Being born again and again,
dying again and again.


6.  Fear
Fear has postponed you,
the good days are not over.

7.  Fear free

Fear or fear-free,
spring will come,
to you and to me.


8.  Crosses

The two crosses stood on the
mountain
and in me,
carry more than one cross,
lose hope or the crosses.


9.  Firm

We hold eternally to the crosses,
they also give an inverted sense.

### 10. Emptiness

Finally found the emptiness
and suddenly discover the crosses
again,
they begin to curse and be determined.


### 11. Wound

Not letting the wound of the heart
heal,
taking care of the wound properly
and letting everything into the heart,
poison and waste.


### 12. Unfortunately

Unfortunately,
the suffering does not always have a
great meaning,
but for the displacement,
the suffering always makes sense.

While I was putting the pages together, I thought about decorating the book with pictures. A few times I did that, then I deleted the pictures again. With the cover picture, it was easy. The image is the reflection in the kitchen cabinet from the dining set at my house. I digitally processed the image. In total, I made a series of 24 images from the base image. I used another image from this series as the cover image in the volume "Poetry".

13.  Trust
Take confidence in thoughts
and make a solid image out of it.


14.  Solidified
The wave hits me
and I realize the solid in me,
protected dull.


15.  Sound
The sounding absolute silence has hit
you briefly
and disappears with the first thought of
success.

16.  Despondent
Change despondency into success
consciousness
and be strong
and win
and kill
and finally be human.


17.  Excited
Excited is not excited
and does not come from somewhere,
but has something to do with
unreasonableness
and invades spontaneously.


18.  Candle
Standing candle-straight
and thinking of straight
and of the candle,
thinking of incredible cheerfulness
and being straight.

19. Apple
I found the apple,
but is already something rotten at the
core.


20. Vomit
The vomit of the friendly drunk smells
sour
and drives away my love of wholeness
and understanding.


21. Dandruff
The shoulders full of hair dandruff
somewhat dampens the feigned
superiority.

22.  Brakes
You brake me with your superiority
and I just keep dreaming of great
possessions
and I'll show you already.


23.  Up
When the door opened
and the great sage entered,
he stumbled stupidly.


24.  Friendly
To be kind again
and to embrace the world worldly
and be mastered.

### 25. Core
The great difference in the core shows
everyone
that there is no difference at all,
we reproduce and die.


### 26. Saying
The good sentence and the good saying
invite you to sit and fly away.


### 27. Balanced
Well balanced sit on the earth
and laugh and lost again,
how is it right,
when you have you again.

28. Hoarfrost

To be very ripe
and to be very rough,
to have lost the beginning
and you give yourself the order to find
the beginning again.


29. Load

The load moves into the earth,
deeper and deeper,
the earth is waiting for you.


30. Sounds

Permeated by the sounds,
by the loud
and even louder sounds
and think
and finally say something clever.

31. Exchange
Exchanging some things,
fluids and thoughts,
feelings and hard knowledge,
beliefs and stubbornness
and oneself.


32. Jumped off
Once more and once more
and then run away or not.


33. Short
Looking at the sun,
of course,
briefly and kindly,
although that already hurts,
praising the sun,
briefly and very kindly.

If you come across this thought, may I share my thought with you. I was just wondering where you are, how you feel when you read the poems and who you are?

34.  Net
Wets the thinkers to examine for
explanations,
for the right sense.


35.  Brutal
Without consideration drink the last sip
and like to be brutal,
this is a timeless good character trait.


36.  Promised
Not having promised anything
and creating the center of the earth in
spite of herd consciousness,
come here and surrender.

### 37. Admonisher
Slowly the admonitions of the
admonisher fade,
the admonisher has become old
and thin,
emaciated he seems.

### 38. Reason
There is no real reason
to accumulate great knowledge.

### 39. Doing
To be completely out of one's mind,
to want to be there for sure,
and to be connected.

40. Happiness
A luck to be there
and to have control over the worlds,
good luck.


41. Order
Getting an order,
carrying it out properly
and being proud like a warrior,
you must be a warrior.


42. Appearance
Stepped up and kicked it all in,
be the exemplary strong one.

43. Miracle
There are no additional miracles after all,
the known ones must suffice.


44. Frame
The frame has a beautiful framing function,
framing hope.


45. Seeing
I couldn't see the sun for luck,
and I rejoiced foolishly.

46. Slowly
Coming back to my senses
and being a tidy person,
strengthening arms
and flexing muscles for joy.


47. Twisted
Have thought too much
and twist the conceit,
nod and affirm,
affirm and think on,
make good.


48. Weekend
A weekend,
an end of year and an end of life,
find everything,
without effort.

49. Noise
The continuous noise in the small head
has become music,
a hiss and clang and be friendly to all,
be good.


50. Pay
All may pay,
no bill remains unpaid,
gifts are dangerous
and happiness will be a bad
punishment.


51. Abbreviation
Since the shortcut became habit,
there is no shortcut,
see an arduous life
through the long ways.

52. Miscalculated
To have calculated well,
to be a clever head,
to have calculated well
and yet miscalculated
and yet a new beginning.


53. Words
There will always be words,
words describing
the whole life.


54. Opened
The rest has opened up,
the restlessness comes again
and everything else is all around,
takes hardly any space,
open up everything.

55.  Ready
Being ready now,
doing the work
and having earned the pleasure through
it,
every day new without thinking much.


56.  Vanity
Grab you by the vanity
and already lost,
fall down.


57.  Shine
And it shines the head,
many believe that they can catch.

58. Love
Love must not be forgotten here,
the one love and the other love,
the imagined love
and the emptied love.


59. Darkness
If you look closely at the plan
and think about the day,
the statement will be spread all over the
world.


60. Exposure
Well,
I found a good invention of life
and wrote down its composition.

My world is small, often thoughtless
and often without hope. And suddenly
everything blossoms and I am
permeated with good thoughts. Then I
think to myself again what thoughts
can do.

### 61. Game
Reinvent the old game,
feel safe
and talk to each other.


### 62. Rain
The raindrops stick to the glass
and the idea sticks to the living
raindrops
and attacks you.


### 63. Illusion
The illusion of realization limits my
good work to be interrupted,
I breathe.

64. Attitude

The tone is subtle,
the attitudes tighten
and the morning sun warms up.


65. Reason

A very good reason to live
is to know better without being caught
by oneself or others.


66. Nose

The direction
to the nose helps to reach
the goal
and die.

67.  Perceive
The smell of the finger
opens a new world.


68.  None
Especially the word "none" has a great content,
so I would like to consider the
beginning of an innocent world.


69.  Convenience
Convenience is a good intention
and will not be lost until the end.

70. Finite

Finite takes us infinitely
and let us reconsider our opinions,
we will gladly accept them.


71. Condition

Performance is important
and then allowed,
so I think a good shock condition
will be ignored.


72. Sun

The sun innocently penetrates
the sunburn.

73. Prosperity
The old man blossoms for a moment,
looks happy,
comes home on the last train,
all seems well.


74. Kill
The fish already stinks
and is hungry.


75. Running
Excited,
everyone runs blindly,
exhales and ages prematurely.

76.  Heart
Now you are hard
and have to endure so much pain
that you can finally go to heaven
and be happy.


77.  Beginning
The train was lost at first,
no one heard noise,
it was not very quiet for years
and at first.


78.  Fact free
I forgot everything
and received an unfounded friendly
request.

79. Speed
Move long distances
until you reach the other person's
head.


80. Sense
The rotation reveals a great mystery
and remains unknown.


81. Hand
If you cling to the enemy's hand
and give up your life without violence,
luck will fly.

82. Glass

The broken glass remained in the idea
and no one expected the end.


83. Food

Get ready to eat,
become an enthusiast,
give more rights to enthusiasts
and great people.


84. Cancel

It was not boring to go to church
and wish something
with the vague idea of the last view.

85. Still
Often righteous people
look uncomfortable
and unjust.


86. Alien
Not in the garden house,
put all secrets in plastic bags
and count on aliens.


87. Right
Wear the right shirt at the right time
and arrive on time for the funeral.

88. Dream
Like the dreams flying in the sky,
the best kind of dream is to wash myself
and breathe the smell of others.


89. Heroes
After receiving the medals,
I can call myself a human being.


90. High
Clouds of the sky seem to fly high,
remembering the past
and laughing with decals.

91. Arbitrary
For good reasons,
the driver could not stop,
every responsibility was with others,
even love was a word.


92. Fast
Birds at the window sing a song
early in the morning.


93. Out
Go, go up,
play in life, go up, go up, go well,
do well.

94. Responsibility
I'll give you the responsibility,
it's not my job at all.


95. Worms
Worms find holes in your mind,
find their home here
and stay with you
for the rest of your life.


96. Heart
I meet my heart,
I meet your heart
with an empty heart,
I meet my presence
with an empty heart.

It is not the end. The end will come in time.